George Curtisius

Peace Solution

for

Ukraine and Iraq/Syria

George Curtisius

Self-Publisher: George Curtisius

Contact: **george.curtisius@web.de**

ISBN-13:978-1507852606

ISBN-10:1507852606

Dedication

I dedicate this booklet to all people, who want to have peace in their own country and who want to live in peace with all followers of Islam and all immigrants.

I also dedicate this booklet to the readers of online articles which have criticized the politics in their comments in a similar or same way like me. I haven't mentioned the unbearable propaganda of the media for the government and their opinion manipulation here. I have this described in detail in my book: "Diktatur des Kapitalismus -- Vision eines modernen Sozialismus" (at present only in German language available).

I thank my dear wife for her suggestions for the title also to single issues and for the examination of the manuscript.

Table of Contents

Preface

I write this booklet under a pseudonym. The reason for this is that I don't want to discuss my views with critics. Who doesn't like my views may be looking for readers of my treatise, which share my views as discussion opponents. Under these readers certainly could be found followers of my theses that are ready to discuss them publicly.

With this brochure I would like to sensitize the readers and particularly the politicians to more political realism. Many conflicts in the world are caused by politicians because they regard national boundaries drawn artificially often as unchangeable.

The politicians ignore, that different ethnic groups of people with their special culture and partly different languages as well as groups of people with a different religion separate each group from the other. There has been oppression in the past. Hatred has arisen if people were killed. Remained have usually insoluble concepts of the enemy.

Despite the arisen and existing conflicts politicians dream, that different ethnic groups having made the other an enemy for years or for decades must cohabit peacefully. But every conflict prevents communities to develop economically well.

My booklet wants to call on politicians to give up their thinking blockades. The politicians are exhorted to create peace instead of solidifying existing conflicts on the basis of self-opinionatedness.

It is a generally accepted right of people to live in freedom and peace. People have the right to live in a community with other people they want to live in, in a community with a value system, which they accept. They are entitled to demand of their government that it doesn't oppress them and that it doesn't go after them.

This booklet is a description of some civil wars and frozen conflicts in Eastern Europe and Middle East.

It also provides suggestions how peace can be achieved.

The content of this booklet is to a large extent identical with the first part of my brochure in German language with title "Friedenslösung für Ukraine, Irak/Syrien – Konflikt-Gefahren durch

Wirtschaftsflüchtlinge und Islam?", which was published December 2014.

My new version in English has been complemented by some new thoughts, which permit politicians the construction of peace in regions where people need peace instead of fear or even war.

The conflicts in Eastern Europe

There is a number of conflicts in Eastern Europe at present. The conflict between the separation endeavors of the Donbas in the eastern Ukraine from remaining Ukraine burdens not only the people living in these regions but also the EU. The sanctions taken by the EU against Russia burden the people in Russia but also the enterprises in the EU with negative consequences for the employees in EU enterprises. Jobs got lost.

Another conflict can be seen in this that the provinces Abkhazia and South Ossetia have themselves separated from Georgia.

Armenia and Azerbijan argue over the enclave lived in by Armenians by the majority, Bergkarabach, on the territory of Azerbijan.

The region Transnistria has itself separated from Moldova.

Kosovo has separated from Serbia and declared its independence. But about 200,000 Serbs still live in the field claimed by Kosovo and want to Serbia. Violence between Serbs and Kosovan Albanians has to be prevented by the Nato troop KFOR.

In Bosnia-Herzegovina three ethnic groups, the Bosnians, the Croatians and the Serbs were combined to an artificial state.

The Bosnians are predominantly Muslims, the Croatians are predominantly Roman Catholic. The Serbs belong predominantly to the Serb Orthodox Church. The state consists of two autonomous regions. The Serb population has their autonomous region and the Bosnians and Croatians are combined in another autonomy. The office of the High Representative for Bosnia and Herzegovina shall provide peace on behalf of UN in the country. How can one approve of such a crooked state construction? The Serbs as enemies of the Bosnians in the Yugoslavia war will block the state politically if always possible. Why doesn't one affiliate the autonomous region of the Serbs to the Republic of Serbia by referendum?

George Curtisius

The Territorial Integrity as a Think Trap

The cause of conflicts is the one-dimensional thinking together with cantankerousness of ministers of the respective governments.

Like-minded politicians in the one-dimensional thinking and cantankerousness support them. It is their self-righteousness to rely on in case of conflict often of great powers artificially drawn borders. In most cases, they also demand the attention of international agreements, statements, memoranda, etc. with respect to territorial integrity. Who insists on dogmatism cannot find new ways of thinking or a different perspective. He finds no solution to problems.

The cause of conflicts, of discord and even wars are the politicians in individual countries, which act over the heads of the people they govern. There are politicians who do not respect the will and the self-determination right of its citizens, for purely political and strategic considerations. On this political level conflicts cannot be resolved. There cannot be any peace there. And the politicians of neighboring countries also prevent the peace so by approving of this politics which disregards the self-determination right of the citizens.

Who owns a territory? The government does not own it, neither politically nor economically. A government only administrates its territory for which it was elected. The people that live and work in a defined area own this territory or parts of a territory in terms of political correctness. And they can in terms of self-determination right decide if their area or part of territory shall belong to the whole territory or not. Politicians have to be aware of the existence of this right. They cannot override that right.

Politicians in the governments have taken an oath to do no harm to their people. However, if their policy is on the political level only based on dogmatism, they add to the inhabitants of damage. They are responsible for the resulting discord, for resulting conflicts.

In order to resolve conflicts peacefully, we need a new approach or perception. From Albert Einstein comes the knowledge that problems cannot be solved on the same level. On the basis of falsity to make more of it, does not resolve the problem.

Einstein realized that problems can only be solved by the next higher level. If politicians want to resolve the conflicts in Eastern Europe and the Middle East, they have to climb up a level! They must rise higher than to persist on the low level of the territorial integrity of dogmatism.

Insisting on the construct of territorial integrity is currently thwarting any possibility of peace.

A territorial integrity shall protect states against the attack of a neighboring state. None of the state's areas shall be taken away or contested. It's about the inviolability of the territory, the acreage or area of a country and its political independence, its state authority

Earlier, when all the people were more or less equally poor, the conquest of the country was important. It was all about for a conqueror to gain agricultural used areas. With more land that could be used for agriculture, yields were connected. It was a precaution against hunger, too. A small wealth could also be achieved.

Hitler's war against the countries of Eastern Europe was based on the idea that the German people need extra space in the east. The two world wars had as a consequence that Germany lost about a third of its previous area.

With about 81 million inhabitants in 2014 in comparison with 1910 with 65 million inhabitants about 24 per cent more German inhabitants live on the smaller area now. But Germany is much richer than at the beginning of the 20th century on a smaller area today. The above figures were taken at Wikipedia.

As a result of World War II Germany lost several provinces, e.g. Pomerania und Silesia. The German inhabitants had fled their territory because of the fights. After the war Polish citizens settled in these former German provinces. Germany accepted the loss of these provinces and the new borders linked with this. Nobody did care about the violation of territorial integrity. The land belonged to the people who were settling there.

Countries with largely predominant production of agricultural products are relatively poor in comparison to industrialized countries. Today a strong industrialization is an important guarantee for the prosperity of the citizens, complemented by a strong service sector.

Agriculture is of minor importance. The differences between rich and poor countries, as per capita income today are many times greater than 100 to 200 years ago.

In Europe, no country will attack another country to gain agricultural land, not even to obtain commodities for themselves.

In former Yugoslavia citizens of different ethnic groups and languages have been united rather forced. That was likewise in the Soviet empire. During the subsequent disintegration of the Union of Soviet Socialist Republics (USSR) this led to problems.

The territorial integrity of the USSR was, strictly speaking, violated when several former Soviet republics declared their independence. The Western countries have kept those violating the territorial integrity of the USSR legitimate. It corresponded to their political interest to weaken Russia.

In most conflicts in Eastern Europe that currently exist, the territorial integrity of states, which have split off from the former Soviet Union, is not threatened from outsides. The threat came from within. Is the internal threat of the territorial integrity as legitimate as the previous secession of the USSR?

Of Georgia the provinces Abkhazia (240,000 inhabitants) and South Ossetia (72,000 inhabitants) have themselves separated. The residents of Russian language and Abkhazian language felt apparently oppressed by the government of Georgia.

Abkhazia has suffered a changeable destiny according to Wikipedia. Georgia occupied Abkhazia with the help of the troops of the German Empire in June 1918. Georgia hurt the territorial integrity of Abkhazia.

Abkhazia became an independent Soviet Republic in 1921. This republic did not press ahead with the collectivization of agriculture as Josef Stalin had demanded. Therefore he made Abkhazia in 1931 to an autonomous republic within the Georgian Soviet Republic. The self-determination of the people was ignored. The territorial integrity of Abkhazia was violated.

In 1992, Abkhazia declared its independence from Georgia after the Abkhazians had been suppressed as a minority of the Georgian government. The Abkhazians have their own language and a different font from the Georgian Cyrillic alphabet.

In Wikipedia, we read that from 1918 to 1920, Georgia conquered the self-governing region of South Ossetia in the Georgian-South Ossetian conflict. So Georgia violated the territorial integrity of South Ossetia. Georgia shall have done genocide to the South Ossetians.

In Wikipedia is to read further, that Georgia was annexed in 1921 by the Soviet Union. 1922 South Ossetia was made by the Soviet Union a part of Georgia. The residents of South Ossetia were not asked whether they agree with it. There was no referendum of South Ossetians for belonging to Georgia. Have Russia's castigators considered this?

After the disintegration of the Soviet Union, the South Ossetians decided several times in referendums their independence from Georgia. Georgia did not recognize the result of these referendums. There were several military struggles between Georgia and South Ossetia. In South Ossetia was stationed under an agreement between Russia and Georgia, a Russian peacekeeping force to separate the fighting parties. In a renewed attack on South Ossetia, Georgia is said to have used cluster bombs against civilians. Members of the Russian peacekeeping force shall have been killed by the military of Georgia.

The 550,000 inhabitants of Transnistria would no longer be represented by the Government of Moldova after the collapse of the Soviet Union. 1990-1992 they separated from Moldova. They declared their independence.

In Ukraine, the Donbas inhabitants in eastern Ukraine do not want to go with the Western Ukraine towards the EU. They don't want to adopt a life of immorality and permissiveness which is usual liberality in the European Union. The approximately 6.5 million residents have opted in two referendums for the independence of Ukraine.

In all the above cases, the territorial integrity not from outside, not from neighboring countries is threatened. Ethnic groups have decided for ethnic and / or linguistic or cultural reasons for a divorce from their previous state. They only make use of their right to self-determination.

The spin-off from their previous state is to compare with the divorce of a marriage. With a divorce is figuratively the "territorial integrity of marriage" hurt if there is something like that at all.

Divorce is independent of the Christian teaching of secular and thus political rights after a period of consideration at any time possible. The divorce cannot and must not be prevented politically.

In a divorce, the two spouses owned assets will be divided. A divorce is a business transaction ultimately. Divorce with separation of assets is ruled by the divorce court and must be accepted by both partners.

The divorce intentions of ethnic groups in different countries should not be judged politically on the basis of territorial integrity therefore, when a referendum justifies the secession. As in a divorce an agreement on the economic impact of such a separation should be made.

A state consists of the people living in this state formation, its inhabitants. The inhabitants entitled to vote elect their government because of their right to self-determination. In the same way ethnic groups, which feel ethnically and linguistically isolated from the other ethnic groups, make use of their right to self-determination. They can request a "divorce" if they feel oppressed or disdained by other ethnic groups. Divorce also is justified when an ethnic group of cultural, ethnic, linguistic, religious or other reasons do not want to go along with the majority of the population.

In a marriage a partner who wants a divorce, cannot be forced to give up the divorce and to continue the marriage compulsorily. The same applies to a minority group in a country, which wants a divorce, as a split-off from the previous state.

If the majority of people in a nation compel with force of arms the minority to remain in the previous state, this causes a conflict. Is the minority armed, so there will be a civil war with many dead and injured and other types of damages. The infrastructure and buildings are mostly destroyed. It ends with a "frozen conflict" if the reconquest is not obtained by the majority.

A "frozen conflict" binds on both sides of staff and financial resources. Both sides have expenses for personnel, weapons and other material. This causes loss of wealth.

If one partner in a marriage the other partner "beats", maybe even "hurts" a cure of the conflict is usually not possible. A divorce is inevitable. This is similar to a situation in which one party to the other party shoots with weapons and members of the other party kills.

If the majority manages to defeat a minority group by force of arms, so that they must remain compulsory in the state of their "oppressors", they are against the state with hatred. What can a state expect or what can a majority of citizens expect from the minority of citizens which meet them with hatred and disgust?

Peace Solution for the Eastern Ukraine

To the opinions of politicians to Ukraine conflict, my wife has a simple picture in mind. The politicians remind her of a pack of dogs that are scrambling in an arena for a gnawed bone. They feel full right.

December 2014, 60 former German politicians and celebrities with their appeal "Again war in Europe?" had demanded to improve relations with Russia. The initiators of the appeal included the former chancellor advisor Horst Teltschik (CDU), the former Defence Secretary Walther Stützle (SPD) and former Vice-President of the Bundestag Antje Vollmer (Green). Even former chiefs of government of the German federal states have signed and the former German Federal President Roman Herzog.

The signatories to the appeal had thus a bone not yet gnawed off thrown to the politicians in the arena. But these politicians insisted to continue to fight over the gnawed bone. They rejected because of dogmatism from each new view of the conflict.

The population of Ukraine has been split for years into a part that tends to the EU and another part that tends to Russia. There was the orange revolution, with which the population got dissatisfied. They elected again. The part of voters tending toward Russia won the majority. They elected their leader Yanukovych as President. Ukraine at that time was actually already bankrupt. The government negotiated with the IMF on the granting of stand-by credits.

The USA (US) and the EU as a helper of the United States strived for years to constrict Russia, to weaken Russia politically and strategically. They actually operated their own expansion against Russia, even if it is now disputed.

Russia offered to Ukraine to participate in Russia's planned Free Trade Area "Eurasia". The US and the EU wanted to prevent the joining of the Ukraine to Eurasia. The EU now offered Ukraine the signing of an association agreement. This agreement would allow Ukraine to access the large Free Trade Area of the EU. President Yanukovych seemed initially leaning toward signing the contract. But then he refused. The EU set then the Ukraine under pressure to conclude the Contract of Association proposed by the EU.

When President Yanukovych still refused, the Maidan-coup occurred. It can be counted on the five fingers of one hand, who in the coup had his hands in the game, who probably has organized and financed the coup.

Undemocratically and using force hundreds of thousands of demonstrators chased the elected president out of his office, allegedly because of corruption.

It is beyond dispute that Ukraine has been plundered by corrupt politicians and oligarchs and kleptocrats since its independence in 1991. In this way it was said in articles in WirtschaftsWoche, including in WiWo of 12-6-2014 ("South Stream – Lieber mit Putin").

The USA (US) and the EU faced the goal of their strategic planning. They saw themselves as the winner. With the process of association of the Ukraine with the EU the US and the EU would gain control of the port of the Russian Black Sea Fleet in Crimea. They could refuse to renew the contract for the stationing of the Russian Black Sea Fleet in Crimea. Russia would have no harbor for its Black Sea fleet more. This plan of US and the EU did not work in the end.

The coup on the Maidan split the country and destabilized the Ukraine. The people in eastern Ukraine did not agree with this coup. The US and the EU, but also the government in Kiev, had not anticipated this resistance.

The inhabitants of the Crimea, which were dissatisfied with the government in Kiev for a long time, made a referendum. More than 90 percent of citizens voted for independence of the Crimea from Ukraine. Subsequently, the parliament of the autonomous region Crimea opted for independence and for an annexation to Russia. The Russian parliament adopted the request of the Crimea to affiliate with Russia.

Principally it was rather a reunification of Russia and the Crimea. But the US, EU and other states did not accept this.

In contradistinction to that reunification of Crimea with Russia there was no referendum, which would have legitimized the German reunification. The cause of the German reunification was demonstrations of several hundred thousand citizens in several towns.

Then the citizens were allowed to leave eastern Germany in order to stay in Western Germany. But there was no referendum held, which would have allowed the 14 million inhabitants of Eastern Germany to approve the reunification with Western Germany. Only the parliament (Volkskammer) of Eastern Germany decided to reunite with Western Germany. The US, EU and all other states accepted this decision and the German reunification.

Western countries measure with double standards if it is strategically an advantage for them. Due to this unreliable behavior the western countries lost their credibility for a long time.

Ukraine protested against the annexation of the Crimea to Russia because the territorial integrity of Ukraine had been violated. The Western countries condemned the violation of the territorial integrity of Ukraine. The US and the EU were now no more the victors of the poker of strategic expansion. They were the losers. The Crimea with the port of the Russian Black Sea fleet was lost for all time to Russia. After the annexation of the Crimea to Russia, the members of the EU had only the pauperized Ukraine around their necks.

Now the EU must support the destitute and by corrupt politicians plundered Ukraine even financially. Presumably, the Ukraine will become financially a bottomless pit for the EU as Greece already is. These failed policies of EU governments are to the detriment of their taxpayers.

With regard to the Crimea, the history should be considered. Since 1783, the Crimea to Russia belonged. Sevastopol in Crimea was build up as the base for the Black Sea Fleet of Russia.

By decision of the Soviet Central Committee (CC) of the CPSU, headed by General Secretary Khrushchev Crimea in 1954 was affiliated to the Ukrainian Soviet Socialist Republic. Virtually with this detachment of the Russian Crimea of Russia and the affiliation to the Ukrainian Soviet Socialist Republic the territorial integrity of Russia got hurt! There was no referendum of the Russian inhabitants of Crimea whether they would now want to be a citizen of Ukraine. Their self-determination rights had been violated. The Western politicians ignore that fact !!!

The Central Committee of the CPSU would have certainly not agreed to the inclusion of the Crimea in Ukraine if it would have to assume that one day Ukraine could no longer be a part of the Soviet empire. The Central Committee under Khrushchev had clearly decided on false assumptions, the inclusion of Crimea in Ukraine.

With a referendum in 1991, Ukraine declared its independence from the former Soviet Union. Strictly speaking they hurt with this decision the territorial integrity of the Soviet Union contributing to its disintegration.

As part of its value system, the US and the EU glorify the right of self-determination of the people. However, the self-determination rights of people accept the governments of the US and the EU countries only in accordance with their strategic calculatio.

They accepted that the inhabitants of Kosovo separate from Serbia in a referendum. They accepted that Serbia's territorial integrity has been violated. In the case of Ukraine, the Crimea and the Donbas, the right of self-determination of people by referendum is not accepted. This is a strange and arbitrary act. How credible are the USA and the EU still?

After the separation of the Crimea from Ukraine the people in eastern Ukraine wanted their independence from Ukraine, too.

Very many years ago the government of the Soviet Union had induced Russian specialists and workers with the promise of higher incomes to go into the Eastern Ukraine. Apparently they had then built the economic center of heavy industry in Ukraine. Therefore, most residents of eastern Ukraine speak Russian and cultivate the Russian values and traditions.

After the coup on the Maidan the newly formed government of Ukraine concluded the association contract with the EU. The Ukraine government stated its intention to want to join the EU. With this intention to join the EU the Russian-speaking citizens of eastern Ukraine did not agree. The residents did not want the EU's decadent value system to take over where morality and ethics can hardly fall even lower. They wanted to continue to live their Russian values and traditions. The decadence of the German value system, as part of the western value system, was described in the German book "Diktatur des Kapitalismus – Vision eines modernen Sozialismus".

Russia tried to mediate. President Putin proposed to give the provinces of Ukraine more autonomy. In particular, the eastern Ukraine should receive greater autonomy. With this it should be alleviated for the Russian-speaking citizens to remain in Ukraine. This Russian proposal met in Kiev and the EU on deaf ears.

People in the oblasts (provinces) Luhansk and Donetsk declared after a referendum in this region their independence as their right of self-determination. They were then regarded as terrorist separatists. The Ukraine government ordered its military to fight against the separatists. The areas of the separatists were shot by the army with grenades and bombs, shot also with banned cluster bombs.

Politicians of the US and the EU seemed to approve the killing of separatists and civilians, women and children, at least by their silence.

The separatists then asked Russia for help.

To my knowledge, there was a peace proposal. It foresaw that the Eastern Ukraine should receive extensive autonomy with its own parliament. This included the requirement that the Eastern Ukraine for three years does not separate from the Ukraine. The Ukraine government would thus have had the opportunity to convince the residents of eastern Ukraine, especially the Donbas, of the benefits of integration into the EU. After three years, the residents of the Donbas should be free to decide whether they want to be independent or to remain in Ukraine with the way to the EU. This peace proposal had no chance. The Kiev government insisted on their purported right to recapture the Donbas area.

To date, more than 5,000 people were killed in the fighting of the conflict parties, injured about 10,000 people. By the bombardment of Luhansk and Donetsk with grenades many buildings, roads, bridges, railways and industrial facilities were destroyed or damaged.

Power and water supply are not or only partially in operation. Coal mines are filled up with water and destroyed by lack of electricity to pump water. The residents of Donbas not yet escaped freeze and starve. Kiev doesn't pay retirees pension anymore. Millions of inhabitants of the Donbas have fled from war. They are now homeless.

The Ukrainian army has a low motivation to fight for the territorial integrity of their country. The motivation has to be improved because many reservist soldiers ran away not to risk their death or their health. A German paper reported that the Ukrainian government promised as reward for the soldiers 2,400 EUR for the destruction of a tank and 6,000 EUR for destruction of a fighting jet.

The separatists have no problem with the motivation of their fighters because they fight for the independence of their Pro-Russian area.

Even if President Yanukovych should have acquired several hundred million US dollars or hryvnia, as it was alleged, so are the economic damages higher in unimaginable way, which have developed after his ouster. The price of the currency has fallen by half. Inflation now reached 20 percent. The military operation against the separatists has cost a lot of money.

The biggest mistake that could make the government in Kiev was to let their military and their volunteer militias shoot on the residents of the Donbas, to kill them. Another mistake was to wreak massive destruction in the Donbas. Thus it has sealed the divorce of Donbas from the rest of Ukraine. There is now no chance that residents of the Donbas want to remain part of Ukraine. The already accomplished separation of the Donbas cannot be undone.

The Nonsense of Sanctions

Of the USA (US) and EU sanctions were imposed against Russia. This is actually a political and an economic war against Russia. Russia should be forced with this economic war to abandon its support for the Pro-Russian separatists in the eastern Ukraine. The goal was to make the separatists give up their separation and make them remain in the Ukraine. The goal was not achieved. For more far-sighted politicians in the West was clear from the very beginning that with sanctions the goal could not be achieved. Sanctions would inflict damage on both sides. But Putin wouldn't be able to let down the Pro-Russian minority in the Donbas. Due to political reasons concerning the expectations of the Russian population he cannot abandon his support of the Pro-Russian separatists.

The sanctions of US and EU have led in a dead end. The Russian government cannot give in with their support of Pro-Russian separatists in Eastern Ukraine. Russia is a powerful state. If it would give in because of the sanctions against its state it would worldwide appear as weak, as a paper tiger. The citizens of Russia would contempt their government.

After having made the grave mistake to impose sanctions on Russia the US and EU cannot take back their sanctions. Otherwise they would appear worldwide as weak.

The US, EU and Russia are caught in a trap. This causes political and economical damages to all parties, as a loss of prosperity. Trade creates prosperity, shrinking trade means less prosperity.

The sanctions of the US and EU against Russia are only of a minor damage to Russia. Russia can endure it for an unlimited time. The longer the western sanctions are in effect the more they invert to an advantage for Russia. In the past Russia had no chance to build up an industry with competitive products that could meet the prices of products imported from EU. Now this chance is given.

As part of the sanctions a lot of EU products are forbidden to export them to Russia. In addition to this the exchange rate of the Rubel has fallen heavily. The prices for imported goods from the EU are accordingly higher. Both has the effect of a protective shield for the Russian industry to be built up.

The sanctions give Russia the chance now to modernize their industry and to build up industries that manufacture up to now imported goods. Russia will become over the years more and more independent of imported goods.

In the meantime Russia aligns its economy more to China. It enlarges the import of goods of China and invites Chinese investors to Russia. Ultimately all these developments as the effect of the sanctions are to the detriment of the industry of the EU. In the long run the EU is the loser.

The power struggle between EU and US on one side and Russia on the other side is to the detriment of the people in the Ukraine. It causes an inconceivable suffering to the people. They have to suffer from this power play when soldiers of the Ukraine army kill separatist fighters and civilians and destroy buildings and infrastructure and when also separatist fighters kill many Ukraine soldiers. What is the sense of this policy? Does it serve humanity? Does it bring peace and freedom? Does it bring security, prosperity and happiness to the people concerned? Have these people concerned a future they can enjoy?

This power play is also of damage to the economical development of Ukraine. Ukraine is a very poor state and nearly bankrupt! A civil war costs a lot of money. It would also be in the interest of Ukraine to end this civil war.

The EU and the Ukraine feels threatened by Russia. They decide to invest a lot of money in new and better weapons. Russia feels threatened by the US, the EU and the Ukraine. It decides to invest a lot of money in new and better weapons. But weapons generate no earnings. They feign security that actually cannot be achieved with this. They are of no advantage for the economy in the long run. How does it make sense to invest in weapons instead of making peace?

The US ambition of predominance over Europe is carried out on the back of the killed soldiers of Ukraine and the killed separatists and civilians. Can the European politicians approve that killing of people in Eastern Ukraine in favor of the goal of the US?

There are demands of the Ukraine to get modern weapons of the USA. The US administration could be willing to supply such weapons and to train Ukrainian soldiers how to use these weapons.

With the supply of modern weapons the US plans to increase their pressure on Russia to withdraw its support of the Pro-Russian separatists. But this undertaking would have grave consequences.

The escalation of the civil war by the US and by the Ukraine government would increase the danger that Russia occupies the whole territory of the Ukraine or at least all 9 provinces (oblasts) of the whole eastern Ukraine.

Russia then would annex the whole eastern Ukraine. This would be more disadvantageous for the government in Kiev as only to grant independence to the two provinces Luhansk and Donezk. Or it could come at least to a "frozen conflict".

Would the US and the EU risk a world war III to free the eastern Ukraine from occupation by Russia? A war between NATO and Russia would take place predominantly on the grounds of Ukraine and the grounds of EU countries with the result of heavy destructions of infrastructure, buildings, enterprises and many thousand dead and crippled people. Who is prepared to bear the responsibility for such war?

Is it not wiser to construct peace with realpolitik instead of increasing the risks of a world war III?

How can the US and EU get out of their self-produced trap? Or shall this conflict become a "frozen conflict" forever?

How could be achieved a Peace Solution now?

The procedure should be like a divorce. The spatial separation of the Donbas of Ukraine has to be accepted. The Donbas with the cities Donetsk and Luhansk obtains independence. The Ukraine, the EU and the US recognize it as an independent state.

It needs to be negotiated on the economic consequences.

It would be conceivable the following solution. Russia reduces its gas price for the Ukraine for the next 10 years by 15 percent. The EU pays a billion EUR to the new state in the Donbas for the reconstruction of plants, which were destroyed by the Ukraine army. Russia contributes with other financial resources in the reconstruction of the Donbas.

The families of civilians killed in the Donbas should each receive compensation worth 20,000 €. The injured civilians and tortured people will each receive compensation in the value of € 10,000. The oligarchs in the Donbas should pay 15 percent of their wealth, spread over 10 years, as a kind of equalization of burdens for the damaged homeowners and owners of small businesses in the Donbas.

For the loss of Crimea, Ukraine does not receive any compensation. The Crimea had never belonged legitimately to the Ukraine, because the inhabitants had never voted – with their right of self-determination - to belong to the Ukraine. The Ukraine government in Kiev had to pay all the years large subsidies for the livelihood of citizens in the Crimea. Without the Crimea Ukraine's financial situation is better.

Russia could possibly agree to grant the Ukraine if it belongs neither to NATO nor to the EU to allow for 10 years to use the naval base in Crimea for the Ukrainian Navy.

The sanctions of USA, EU and other countries against Russia should be repealed. Likewise, Russia's sanctions against the US and the EU have to be lifted.

Peace for Georgia and Renegade Provinces

In Abkhazia and South Ossetia ethnic groups live that do not fit ethnically to Georgia. They want nothing to do with Georgia. Again, there is a divorce. Georgia must recognize this divorce intention. Relative to about 4.5 million people in Georgia are the 240,000 Abkhazians and 72,000 South Ossetians economically insignificant. Their separation should not justify any economic compensation.. Otherwise the losses, which have resulted for the renegade provinces by warlike actions of the Georgian government, also would have to be offset.

It is a matter of prudence, to terminate such minor conflicts.

Abkhazia and South Ossetia should be granted independence from Georgia. Without termination of these conflicts Georgia has no chance of ever becoming a member of NATO or even the EU.

The governments in the EU should urge Georgia to grant the independence of Abkhazia and South Ossetia. What these states then do with their independence should be up to them.

Peace in Moldova and Transnistria

Already during the dissolution of the Soviet Union in 1990-1992 Transnistria had split-off from Moldova. Since that time, there is a "frozen conflict". According to Wikipedia, the citizens of Transnistria in 2006 voted in a referendum by a very large majority for independence from Moldova and for an accession to Russia.

Here is a clear finding of a divorce. You cannot force the 550,000 citizens of Transnistria to a reunion with Moldova. On both sides of the conflict armed forces are in standby. In a peace treaty, the number of unproductive military and the expenditure for armed forces can be reduced significantly.

Moldova should recognize the independence of Transnistria, mediated by the EU. There should be a peace treaty concluded. If it is to negotiate economic compensation, the damage should be taken into account, which has added the military of Moldova to Transnistria.

Peace Solution for Serbia and Kosovo

The Kosovo originally belonged to the Federal Republic of Yugoslavia. After 2003, it was a partial region of the Republic of Serbia. To be read in Wikipedia. The inhabitants of Kosovo practice Islam as a religion. The majority of Serbs belong to the Serbian Orthodox Church, they are Christians.

The Kosovo War of 1999, eventually has had as a result that the Kosovo declared independence from Serbia 2008. The self-determination right of the Kosovo Albanians was recognized. The US and the EU accepted the violation of the territorial integrity of Serbia.

But there are still conflicts between the Serbs living in northern Kosovo and Kosovo Albanians. The NATO force KFOR may not even prevent these conflicts. The dispute is the result of oppression in the past. Previously, Serbia had Kosovo Albanians suppressed. Now the Kosovars suppress the Serbian minority living in their territory. By warlike actions where people were killed, hatred arose.

This hatred and the much earlier developed enemy images because of different ethnicities and different religions cannot be removed with a little democracy-color. Who does believe this, doesn't know any about realpolitik.

This conflict is typical of the policy pursued by the US, the UN and the governments of the EU. It is the goal of these countries and the UN primarily to maintain once existing state structures. The US, the EU and the UN do not care about the fate and the will of the people in countries with different ethnic groups that fight against each other that don't fit to each other. This policy is inhumane. This policy is forcing people to live in the same territory, although they do not want that and although they experience all days their aversion, their hatred, against the other ethnic group.

The US, EU and UN insist on the conservation of an arbitrarily defined area without regarding the will and the interests of people living in this area.

The Serbians living in the north of Kosovo at the border to Serbia don't accept the independence of Kosovo. They do not want to be ruled by Kosovo Albanians. If it is true that the Kosovo government is controlled by organized crime, it certainly cannot be expected by the Serbs to be governed by the Kosovars.

Living in northern Kosovo Serb minority wants to belong to Serbia. But their self-determination right is not recognized. Why the double standards?

What sense does it make to want to prevent disputes between the ethnic group of the Serb minority in Kosovo and the ruling Kosovo Albanians with an international force? Should this force be stationed until 2100 and possibly longer there?

The conflict situation can only be terminated by the international community with Serbia and Kosovo by agreeing that the north of Kosovo, where Serbs are in the majority, is affiliated to the Republic of Serbia. Then there is a clear boundary between the ethnic Serbs and ethnic Albanians of Kosovo. Problems with smaller minorities can be solved also.

The international community must respect that the self-determination rights of the people are of higher rank than territorial boundaries or territorial integrity.

Peace for Iraq and for Syria

In the Sykes-Picot agreement of May 16th, 1916, England and France agreed on their zones of influence in Middle East. Borders could be established freely in every influence zone. So it has to be read in Wikipedia.

It is claimed by the representatives of the Islamic State that for the Sunnites the borders were established artificially for Iraq and for Syria. They did not meet tribal affiliations, not their ethnicity, not their kind of Islam.

In the Iraq of Saddam Hussein about 60 percent of the population belonged to the Shia faith of Islam. They lived mostly in the south of Iraq around the city of Basra.

About 20 percent of residents were Sunni Arabs. They mostly inhabited the area around the city of Fallujah. About 10 percent were Sunni Kurds. They inhabited the north of Iraq.

There were also Christians in Iraq. Under Saddam Hussein as president Christians were represented in its government.

The Sunnites as Arab minority ruled as Baath Party under Saddam Hussein the country. The Shiites and Sunni Kurds were suppressed. Shiite uprisings with at least 30,000 dead people were the result. The Kurds complained a lot more dead bodies. Against them even poison gas was used by Saddam Hussein.

The Kurds succeeded to achieve a limited autonomy for their Kurdish region.

After the Iraq war (2003 - 2011), Iraq was politically destabilized. The majority of Shiites took power. Now the Arab Sunnis were oppressed with their settlement area in the region Fallujah. They defended themselves with explosives attacks and suicide bombings against Shiites.

Conversely, the Shiites committed explosive attacks on Sunnites. There were many thousands of dead people and injuries on both sides. That enlarged still the hatred on their long-standing enemy.

But parts of the power supply, water supply and oil pump stations were repeatedly damaged by explosives attacks and disabled.

Especially at the example of Iraq it can be perceived what the enemy images have as an effect.

You cannot force people to live against their will in a state in which they do not want to live on religious or ethnic reasons. This only causes uprisings or even civil war with many dead persons.

Western governments believe that the unity of a country is more important than the religious or ethnic influenced will of the people in a country. Following the example of their secular oriented countries where different religions and ethnic groups live together in peace, they think that this also must be possible in the Arab countries. This is a big mistake and far removed from realpolitik.

In Iraq under Saddam Hussein, the minority Sunnis oppressed the majority Shiites.

After the death of Saddam Hussein, the majority of Shiites suppressed the Sunnis. Many thousands of people killed by terrorist attacks were and are the consequence. The Christians were persecuted, so they had to leave the country.

In Syria, the majority of the Sunni population rose against the elected Assad regime in Damascus, which is formed substantially from the minority Alawite, a Shiite branch of Islam. More than 160,000 dead people now caused the civil war. The jihadists joined the Sunni Syrians in their fight against the Assad regime. It has been presumed so far that the Syrian Sunnis practice a moderate form of Islam.

The jihadists practice a fundamentalist Islam under reference to the Koran. They want to establish a caliphate, a God-state. It is argued that the Syrian rebels and the jihadists from Saudi Arabia and Qatar are financed. Both governments deny that. However, they admit that rich individuals from their countries finance these rebels.

Saudi Arabia propagates the Wahhabi Islam, a devout Sunni branch of Islam. To this direction belong the Salafists. This direction of Islam considers the Shia Islam as nonbelievers. They may be killed, as well as the Sunni Kurds, Alawites, Yazidis and Christians.

In addition to the struggle for religious supremacy Saudi Arabia wants to overthrow out of political reasons the democratically elected Alawite Assad government in Damascus. The Assad regime is supported by the Shiite Iran. On the Arabian Peninsula, however, only Saudi Arabia wants to exercise influence.

It's in the fight against the Assad regime is not a struggle against the dictator Assad. It isn't all about a fight against the dictator Assad at the fight against the Assad regime. Even Saudi Arabia is a dictatorship, as well as the oil sheikhdoms. It is a religious war against the Alawites and Shiites.

Would the Sunni rebels and the jihadists win this religious war, they would slaughter many tens of thousands of Alawites as infidels. Millions of Alawites were fleeing. Many thousands of these refugees would flock to Germany and other European countries.

In 2014, the jihadists have conquered large parts of Syria and Iraq. They have founded the Islamic State (IS) and proclaimed a caliphate. This conquest was only possible because many Arab Sunnis of Iraq have joined the jihadists. These Iraqis were former officers and soldiers of Saddam Hussein and were Sunni tribal warriors.

The Islamic State (IS) has committed terrible crimes against people. Western journalists were beheaded. Tribal leaders and residents of tribes that were not obedient were killed. There were mass executions. Shiites, Yazidi, Kurds and Christians were killed, as well as moderate Sunni Muslims.

The Iraqi government of Shiites together with the Kurds fight against the Islamic State. Many Sunni fighters from western countries joined the Islamic State because of its cruelty against its enemies. It is reported that more than 5,000 combatants should have joined the IS.

The Western world supports Iraq in the war on IS. It provides weapons and instructs the Iraqi army. With air strikes against the IS supporting the Kurds and the Iraqi army. The Western world thinks to be able to totally destroy the IS. One believes that one can restore the rule of the Shiite government over the whole territory of Iraq. This is an error! It contradicts all realpolitik.

The Iraqi Sunnis will never go back under the rule of the Shiites. The Shiite Iraqi army is poorly motivated to regain Sunni settlements for their government. The Sunni neighbors Saudi Arabia and Jordan have no interest in strengthening the Shiite government in Baghdad. They can also use therefore no ground troops against the IS, because they fear that large parts of their soldiers go over to the IS. The IS with its fundamentalist Islam attracts poor Sunni Muslims. In addition, the IS pays its fighters better than do the other armies. Saudi Arabia and Jordan on the other hand want to see destroyed the IS, so that the caliphate of jihadists doesn't threaten their rule.

Without the use of ground forces of Western states in addition to poorly motivated Iraqi army, the IS cannot be defeated.

The Western States are not entitled to intervene with ground troops in Iraq and Syria in the religious wars taking place there. One may imagine the outcry in America, if, for example, American soldiers are captured from the IS and then beheaded publicly. Such a risk the United States won't take.

As long as the Iran, Russia and the Hezbollah militia in Lebanon support the Assad regime, it is not possible to eliminate the Assad regime. The Assad regime is the lesser evil compared with the IS. Under Assad all religions could live together in peace. Among the jihadists and the supposedly moderate Syrian Sunnis peace between all religions will not be possible or no longer be possible. Even the supposedly moderate Syrian Sunnis killed Christians.

In Syria, about three million people have escaped from the civil war and from the jihadists. In Iraq, about one and a half million people are on the run from the Shiite government and from the jihadists. If the religious and ethnic civil wars continue for longer, the number of refugees will enlarge. There is no chance that the refugees can return to their homeland.

Iraq and Syria, as well as the neighboring countries of Iran, Saudi Arabia and Jordan, as well as Western countries would be well advised to seek a peaceful solution to end the wars of religion. Many years or even decades of wars and the suffering associated with it don't have to be expected of the people concerned and the world.

Peace in Iraq and Syria can only be achieved if one separates the religious groups so that they can live in their own state.

If Western leaders believe that in the future Sunni Iraqis will accept to live under the rule and reign of Shia Iraqis again, they are dreamers. They should not believe the protestations of Sunni MPs. These do not want to lose their good pay as Members of Parliament only.

Steps to Peace:

The World Security Council and the UN must be prepared to allow the divide of countries in which take place civil wars on the basis of religious antagonisms and enemy images by negotiations among the warring parties. The same has to be considered for the striving for independence of the Kurds, which are ethnically distinct from other ethnic groups in Iraq and Syria.

Iraq

Negotiators of the World Security Council should explore first whether there is a chance to separate the formerly moderate Sunni Arabs in Iraq (Fallujah region) of the fundamentalist jihadists. They must negotiate with the military leaders of the moderate Sunnis in Iraq (Fallujah region) and with the Sunni tribal leaders, which currently let their warriors fight together with the jihadists. If they can promise the moderate Sunnis that they will get their own state if they separate themselves from the jihadists, they will be ready to withdraw their fighters from the group of jihadists.

On the international level would then be in negotiations with the Shiites in Iraq and the Sunnis and the Kurds to agree on a division of the existing state Iraq, which now no longer exists. For the Kurds, the desire for a separate state is ethnically motivated, less religious.

If the Kurds, Sunnis and Shiites manage respectively their own oil field in their own territory then separated from each other territory and earn on oil exports, the viability is assured for each of these new state structures, too.

With the division of Iraq into three new state structures the wars of the Sunnis and Shiites end against each other. Kurdish uprisings against the Baghdad government are unnecessary. The Baghdad airport could be used potentially in terms of costs both Shiites and Sunnis.

In the negotiations, the jihadists must be granted as a state, a small region in Syria. Shiites and Sunnis and Kurds in Iraq would give them no opportunity to reside there any longer in Iraq.

It could be that it is not possible to assign each of the three successor states of Iraq it's own oil fields. In this case, it has to be considered whether all the oil fields and refineries in all three successor states are put under international administration. The profits from the crude oil production and processing have to be divided up according to the number of inhabitants on the three new territories.

This peace settlement can be reached, if it is possible to separate the moderate Sunnis of the jihadists. The jihadists would have to agree. Otherwise, the moderate Iraqi Sunnis, Kurds and the Iraqi Shiite military would antagonize them. I a fight on three fronts, the jihadists had no chance to survive.

If it would not be possible to separate the moderate Iraqi Sunnis and the Sunni tribal fighters from the jihadists, it is more difficult to achieve peace.

From the conquered territories of the jihadists in Iraq should be separated with the help of the Kurds and the Iraqi army that part in which have been living the Sunnis or can live in the future. This part should become a small Sunni state for perhaps 2 to 3 million Iraqi Arabs. In this state moderate Sunni Iraqis can live who do not want to live under the cruel rule of the jihadists and not under the rule of the adversary Shiites. To achieve this, the Kurds and the Iraqi army would have to get help from the Free Syrian Army (FSA). The western countries would contribute its share of military aid. Overall, it would be the worse alternative.

Possibly there have to be made relocation to separate warring populations from each other. In the Arab world, lasting peace can only be achieved by separation of the enemies, not with appeals or the hope that reconcile enemies again. Saudi Arabia, the oil sheikhdoms and the UN could pay for the costs of resettlement.

Syria

In Syria, the civil war is to end only by a divide of the country.

Russia currently supports the Assad regime, which protects the life of the Alawites and other Shiites. The rebel Free Syrian Army and the jihadists are funded by the Saudis and the oil sheikhdoms, but probably also by the US and the EU. The goal of the US and the EU is to overthrow the Assad regime so that the Syrian port of Latakia can no longer be used of Russia for its ships in the Mediterranean.

In the shade of a religious war initiated by Saudi Arabia the US and EU also pursue the strategic goal to drive Russia away from Syria to eliminate Russia's presence in the Mediterranean Sea and to weaken Russia.

Do the US and the EU actually finance Syrian terrorists who are fighting against the elected government of Assad? If this is the case, they also bear responsibility for the suffering of the people of Syria. They would then also be partly responsible for the refugee flows so that they must likewise provide funds and receive refugees. How prudent would be co-financing of the Syrian terrorists to fight against a democratically elected government? In any case, the initial rebellion was directed against a democratically elected government.

The political-religious war being fought on the backs of innocent Syrians can last indefinitely as long as the funds for the rebels and the Assad regime flow and both sides receive enough weapons.

At the international level it has to be agreed upon with the warring parties, the former Syria, which now no longer exists undivided to divide as part of realpolitik in three countries. The Assad regime is to allot with Damascus and around the port of Latakia a region in which the Alawites and Shiites live. The port of Latakia is also used by Russia. Russia will not give up this right.

The Alawites had, according to Wikipedia, before the civil war a population share of 12 percent, the Christians of about 10 percent. In addition there are shares for Shiites.

Without the participation of Russia in these negotiations it won't be possible to reach an agreement.

George Curtisius

Another part of the former Syria is to assign Syrian Sunnis, with the center of e.g. Aleppo. A third, very small part would be to leave the jihadists, because otherwise there would be no way of where the original 15,000 to 25,000 fighters of the jihadists can withdraw. In addition, all previous financiers of the jihadists would have to cease their financing of the group. Then would dissolve with time this grouping because citizens would escape this reign of terror. And only of fighters no state structure can exist.

In Syria, too, the inhabitants of the three successor states have to receive a fair share of the revenues from oil production and processing.

Task of the international community

Only with the partition of Iraq and Syria to individual countries for religious groups and the Kurds violence between religious groups and the Kurds will end. If you want to believe that peaceful coexistence - without despotic dictatorship – of different religious groups must be possible will act against any realpolitik. He acts also with a lack of understanding regarding the various faiths in Islam. And he underestimates the will of Saudi Arabia to spread their fundamentalist Islam in the region and in the world, also especially in Africa.

To this extent, Lebanon is not an exemplar, if you look at the recent civil wars and the fragile peace between religious groups and that in Beirut Sunni districts are fighting against Shiite neighborhoods.

It is up to countries such as Germany and the permanent members of the World Security Council to take the initiative for peace in Iraq and Syria.

Epilogue

Is the evil in the world, the caste of politicians? The fact is probably that politicians with their neoliberalism create more rich people and enlarge the army of the poor. With their stereotyped patterns of thinking politicians often prepare the ground for conflicts.

Where they could bring peace or would have to do or where they could contribute to peace, they do not do it often enough. There are mental blockades in the way, as the territorial integrity. It will not be asked what is the will of the people and how they want to live. Results of referenda will be swept aside if they do not suit the politicians. Then referenda are called illegal. Thus politicians become responsible for conflicts or at least peace preventers.

Actually, we do not need such politicians. The will of the citizens defying arrogance of politicians caused a great lack of interest for politics. The politicians forget that they represent only a small part of the population with their voters.

I prefer as policy system a government of technocrats, as I have described it as vision of a modern socialism in my German book "Diktatur des Kapitalismus – Vision eines modernen Sozialismus".

Politics is a dirty business, if the established parties defame and slander each other of professional jealousy. Their policy is even more dirty and yet unethically if they approve tacitly a civil war on the ground of Europe with many people killed which they could end if they would respect the self-determination rights of people concerned. If these politicians are of Christian belief they should consider that they make themselves guilty before God.

These "bellicose" politicians can bring peace in a nation with their way of thinking hardly. Who can show esteem and respect to this unethical politicians? Can they promote trustworthily peace in their country?

The politicians of all countries are therefore called upon to behave ethically in the future. They are called to respect the will of the citizens and not to rule over their head. Do not try to force people to a life that they do not want. Politicians should devote themselves without thinking barriers for peace in Europe and among our neighbors. To contribute to peace they should step to a higher level and seek solutions for peace from this higher level instead to insist on their previous demands.

Politicians work hard so they say. But don't they work primarily for their own party career, for the interests of their party members for their re-election? So they do not work first for the welfare of citizens? Aren't they open for being influenced by lobbyists of the great business as to their decisions at the detriment of citizens? Are they not by too many business lobbyists manipulated in their decisions, to the detriment of citizens? Aren't they primarily pure egoists first concerned about their own welfare rather than servants of the people? It's up to the politicians to question their behavior and their decisions, if all of them serve the welfare of the citizens.

Some Thoughts for reflection

It can't be ignored that the administration of the great power USA strives to keep up their long-standing dominance over Europe. The USA influence and dominate the decisions of the Commission of EU.

The US government dominates especially Germany with the German government as their protectorate.

To maintain their supremacy as the dominant global power the US must prevent that the EU works closely together with Russia. The Ukraine conflict is a wonderful occasion to drive a wedge between EU and Russia.

A very close collaboration of the EU with Russia on all political, social, economical and military fields with friendly relations to each other would be a threat to the supremacy of the US. Therefore it has to be understood that the US takes influence on the politicians of the EU on all levels. The NSA spying program collects all data of communications in the EU to know in time what people and politicians might intend.

The strategic partnership between the US und the EU means that the US administration defines or decides the strategy and the EU has to execute this strategy even if it is of detriment to the EU and its population.

It can't be ignored that the USA is not only a strategic partner but also a competitor economically.

Books of George Curtisius

In 2013 George Curtisius published his book trilogy:

"Das FBI gegen die Macht des Gebets",

as a Print version at Amazon as well as Kindle edition, digital also with epub dealers.

The book trilogy is a Christian thriller. People can get happier and more successful with the power of the prayer and the power of the forgiveness. The book contains criticism of the politics and the society of the USA, criticism of capitalism. But also something in this book is satire.

December 2014, George Curtisius published his brochure at Book on Demand:

"Diktatur des Kapitalismus - Vision eines modernen Sozialismus".

The brochure can be bought at all booksellers also at Amazon.

The little book with 92 sides consists of three parts. The dictatorship of the capitalism is described first and how it has an effect on people. Our form of government is a pseudo-democracy. Morals and customs are dilapidated. Part 2 describes the failure of the German Democratic Republic (DDR) with its socialism and the reasons for it.

Part 3 develops the vision of a socialism going out of old ideas into a modern socialism with freedom, peace, justice and far-reaching equality of the living conditions for all citizens, job guarantee and social and personal safety. All citizens live in a modest prosperity. There isn't any poverty.

December 2014 George Curtisius published at Book on Demand his book:

„Friedenslösung für Ukraine, Irak/Syrien! – Konflikt-Gefahren durch Wirtschaftsflüchtlinge und Islam?"

www.ingramcontent.com/pod-product-compliance
Lightning Source LLC
Chambersburg PA
CBHW070513290526
45790CB00003B/1213